CELEBRATING THE CITY OF PUNE

Celebrating the City of Pune

Walter the Educator

Silent King Books
A WhichHead Entertainment Imprint

Copyright © 2024 by Walter the Educator

All rights reserved. No part of this book may be reproduced in any manner whatsoever without written per- mission except in the case of brief quotations embodied in critical articles and reviews.

First Printing, 2024

Disclaimer

This book is a literary work; the story is not about specific persons, locations, situations, and/or circumstances unless mentioned in a historical context. Any resemblance to real persons, locations, situations, and/or circumstances is coincidental. This book is for entertainment and informational purposes only. The author and publisher offer this information without warranties expressed or implied. No matter the grounds, neither the author nor the publisher will be accountable for any losses, injuries, or other damages caused by the reader's use of this book. The use of this book acknowledges an understanding and acceptance of this disclaimer.

Celebrating the City of Pune is a little collectible souvenir book that belongs to the Celebrating Cities Book Series by Walter the Educator. Collect them all and more books at WaltertheEducator.com

USE THE EXTRA SPACE TO TAKE NOTES AND DOCUMENT YOUR MEMORIES

PUNE

In the heart of Maharashtra, where the Mula and Mutha converge,

Celebrating the City of Pune

Lies Pune, a city where histories and futures merge.

Ancient roots entwine with modern dreams so bright,

In this realm of wisdom, where day kisses night.

Beneath the shadow of Sinhagad, legends breathe,

Warrior spirits, in every rustling leaf,

Shivaji's valor, tales of strength and might,

In every stone and whisper, in the moon's soft light.

On bustling streets where rickshaws hum their tune,

A kaleidoscope of colors, under the sun and moon.

Markets buzz with spices, rich and aromatic,
Celebrating the City of
Pune

Lives interwoven, both simple and dramatic.

Fergusson College stands, with its grand, timeless grace,

Nurturing minds, in this scholarly place.

Young hearts on campus, dreaming vast and wide,

Where knowledge and curiosity, harmoniously collide.

In the gardens of Shaniwar Wada, whispers of the past,

Echo through corridors, built to last.

Maratha pride, in each arch and each wall,

A fort of dreams, where memories call.

The Osho Ashram, a sanctuary serene,

Where souls find solace, in the green.

Mystic meditations, under the banyan's embrace,

In this haven of peace, they find their place.

The hills of Parvati, where dawn breaks anew,

With temples that touch the sky, in hues of blue.
Celebrating the City of
Pune

Devotees climb, in silent, sacred tread,

Towards the divine, with prayers softly said.

Pune's rhythms pulse with youthful zest,

In the cafés and clubs, where the city's at its best.

A tapestry of cultures, woven tight,

In laughter and song, through the deep, starry night.

At Aga Khan Palace, history's heavy weight,

Gandhi's spirit lingers, in this solemn state.

A beacon of freedom, in walls so revered,

Where the cries of the past, can still be heard.

Bakeries waft with the scent of fresh pav,

In Irani cafés, with their timeless allure and vow.

Conversations spill over chai and bun maska,

Moments shared in the heart of Pune's saga.

Koregaon Park's lanes, where art meets life,
Celebrating the City of
Pune

With murals and markets, free from strife.

An enclave of peace, amidst the city's hum,

Where creativity's whispers, beckon and come.

Through monsoon showers, the city blooms anew,

Pune's spirit, resilient and true.

ABOUT THE CREATOR

Walter the Educator is one of the pseudonyms for Walter Anderson. Formally educated in Chemistry, Business, and Education, he is an educator, an author, a diverse entrepreneur, and he is the son of a disabled war veteran. "Walter the Educator" shares his time between educating and creating. He holds interests and owns several creative projects that entertain, enlighten, enhance, and educate, hoping to inspire and motivate you. Follow, find new works, and stay up to date with Walter the Educator™

at WaltertheEducator.com

www.ingramcontent.com/pod-product-compliance
Lightning Source LLC
LaVergne TN
LVHW010618070526
838199LV00063BA/5192